SCIENCE Q&A

SPACE SCIENCE

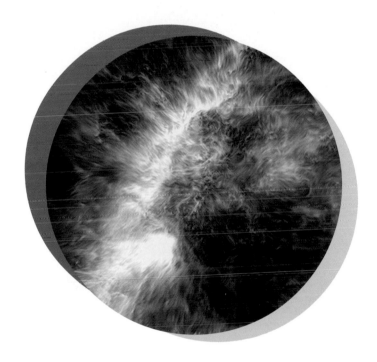

Cavendish Square

New York

Published in 2016 by Cavendish Square Publishing, LLC
243 5th Avenue, Suite 136, New York, NY 10016

© 2016 Brown Bear Books Ltd

First Edition

Website: cavendishsq.com

CPSIA Compliance Information: Batch #WS15CSQ

Library of Congress Cataloging-in-Publication Data

Space science / edited by Tim Harris.
   p. cm. — (Science Q&A)
Includes index.
ISBN 978-1-50260-613-6 (hardcover) ISBN 978-1-50260-612-9 (paperback)
ISBN 978-1-50260-614-3 (ebook)
1. Space sciences — Juvenile literature. I. Harris, Tim. II. Title.

QB500.22 H37 2015
500.5—d23

For Brown Bear Books Ltd:
Editors: Tracey Kelly, Dawn Titmus, Tim Harris
Designer: Mary Walsh
Design Manager: Keith Davis
Editorial Director: Lindsey Lowe
Children's Publisher: Anne O'Daly
Picture Manager: Sophie Mortimer

Picture Credits:
T=Top, C=Center, B=Bottom, L=Left, R=Right

Front Cover : All pictures NASA GRIN/NIX.
Inside: NASA: APOD/NOAO/AURA/NSF 6tr, Apollo Gallery 18r, 19t, 19b, 21tr, ESA 26cl, GRIN 26b, JPL, 5tl, 14tl, 15cr; Mt Palomar Observatory 9r, NIX 4, 5br, 6-7, 8cl, 9l, 10tl, 14b, 18tl, 23tr, 23b, 26tl, 27; Shutterstock: 11b, Benintende 11t, Marcel Clemens 7tr, Byron W Moore 15t, Jurgen Ziewe 10tr; Thinkstock: FAE 22bl, Hemera 22tl, iStockphoto 1, 6t, Photos.com 22r.

Brown Bear Books has made every attempt to contact the copyright holder.
If you have any information please contact licensing@brownbearbooks.co.uk

Printed in the United States of America

CONTENTS

—INTRODUCTION—

The universe is a vast and awesome place made up of billions of stars, galaxies, planets, nebulae, black holes, and other space phenomena. Our planet— Earth—is just a tiny part of the whole picture.

Walk outside on a clear, dark night and look up at the sky. What can you see? Perhaps there is a bright full moon rising above the horizon. Maybe you can see an array of glistening stars, nestled together in groups called constellations. Perhaps you can make out one of the planets—bold Jupiter, dazzling Venus, or reddish Mars— or beautiful "shooting stars" that dart across the sky in a meteor shower. But what are these celestial objects made of, and how did they form? Scientists believe that the universe and everything in it was created after an explosion called the big bang, which happened circa 13.8 billion years ago.

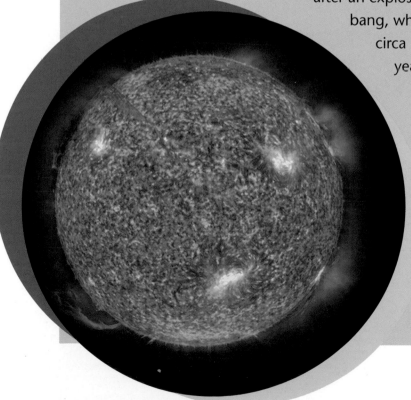

◀ The sun is a star at the center of our solar system. It is orbited by Earth, the planets, and their moons. Without the light and heat given off by the sun, life could not exist on Earth.

◀ The planet Saturn is one of four "gas giant" planets in our solar system. It is circled by rings made up of millions of lumps of rock and ice.

In this book, you will learn about the universe and our solar system—the sun and eight planets: Mercury, Venus, Earth, Mars, Jupiter, Saturn, Uranus, and Neptune—as well as Earth's moon and the fascinating moons orbiting other planets. But astronomy is not a new science: You'll also hear about our ancestors' exploration of the heavens, from ancient Greek and Sumerian astronomers to modern-day physicists such as Albert Einstein.

You'll explore telescopes trained on deep space objects, and NASA's Apollo rockets, which landed the first people on the moon. Finally, you'll discover details about the exciting missions of today—the International Space Station, and space probes that travel to the edge of the solar system.

▶ The International Space Station orbits Earth to collect data and to test equipment for future space missions.

THE UNIVERSE

The universe is thought to be about 13.8 billion years old, the result of a massive explosion called the "big bang."

Scientists still do not know how big the universe really is—but they do know that it is expanding. The universe contains vast numbers of stars, planets, comets, and smaller icy and rocky debris. It also contains large quantities of gases, especially hydrogen and helium.

Stars

Most of the objects in space that we can see are stars. A star is a mass of gas held together by its own gravity. The center of a star is very hot and gives out heat and light. Stars are fueled by nuclear fusion reactions, which change hydrogen to helium.

Stars come in different sizes, colors, and temperatures. Our sun is classed as a yellow star because it is medium sized. The hottest stars (for instance, Zeta Orionis) shine with a bluish light, and the biggest are red supergiants. Canis Majoris, which has a diameter two thousand times larger than the sun's, is a red supergiant.

Galaxies

Stars are usually grouped into galaxies, and there are probably more than eighty billion galaxies in the observable universe. Each is made up of many stars, from ten million in dwarf galaxies to one trillion in big galaxies, making an estimated total of 3×10^{23} stars. Our own solar system is a tiny part of the huge Milky Way galaxy.

▲ The Carina Nebula is a vast area of gas and stars, including some very large stars.

▶ Our own galaxy, the Milky Way, is visible on a clear night. It contains 200 billion to 400 billion stars.

LIGHT YEARS

Distances between objects in the universe are often vast. That is why they are usually given in light years rather than miles (or kilometers). A light year is the distance light travels in one year. It is equal to nearly 6 trillion miles (9.5 trillion kilometers). The brightest star visible from Earth is Sirius, which is 8.6 light years away. The Orion Nebula, sometimes visible with the naked eye, is 1,344 light years away.

Nebulae

The universe also contains nebulae. These vast clouds of dust and gas are places where stars are made. Dust and gas join together to form bigger and bigger bodies. Eventually these may be big enough to make stars, and the material left over may form planets and other rocky bodies.

Planets

Since planets do not give off light and are relatively small, we probably know of only a tiny fraction of the total. Smaller fragments of ice, dust, and rocky particles orbit our sun—sometimes forming comets and meteors—and probably exist in other galaxies.

▲ Halley's Comet comes close to Earth every seventy-five years.

Black Holes

Black holes form in places where stars have collapsed in on themselves. There, the gravitational pull is so strong that nothing can escape—not even light. There is a giant black hole at the center of the Milky Way. Scientists still have a lot to learn about black holes.

GENERAL INFORMATION

● Our own galaxy, the Milky Way, measures about 100,000 light years across.

● It has been estimated that there are 3×10^{23} stars in the universe.

● Three-quarters of the atoms in space are hydrogen.

Q How did the sun and planets form?

A Nobody knows for sure. Most scientists think that the sun, Earth, and other planets (the solar system) were formed from a mass of dust and gas. Nearly five billion years ago, this mass started to shrink, then spin and flatten into a disk. The center of the disk spun fastest. This became the sun. The rest of the material turned into the planets (below).

Q What is a meteor?

A A meteor is a piece of rock from outer space that enters Earth's atmosphere. The friction causes it to burn up. It is seen as a sudden streak of light (above).

Q What is a nebula?

A A nebula is a cloud of dust and gas in space. Some of the clouds block out the light from the stars behind. These are called dark nebulae. One of the best known is the Horsehead Nebula (right). Other dust clouds reflect the light from the stars and shine brightly. These are called bright nebulae.

Q What is a black hole?

A Sometimes—no one knows why—stars collapse in on themselves. This increases their gravity (a force that pulls everything inward). Nothing escapes—not even light. These very dense bodies are called black holes (below).

Q What is a galaxy?

A A galaxy (below) is a huge spinning mass of stars in outer space. There are millions of galaxies, each containing millions or billions of stars as well as gas and dust. Our galaxy, the Milky Way, contains 200 billion to 400 billion stars.

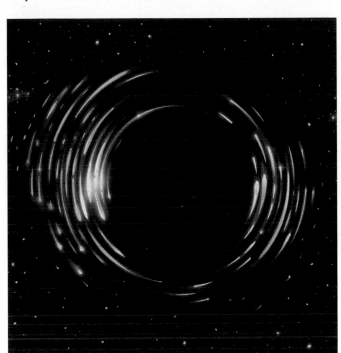

Q How did the universe begin?

A Many scientists believe that all the material of the universe was once crammed together in one place. Then, about 13.8 billion years ago, an explosion, or "big bang," occurred. The material of the universe flew out in all directions, forming galaxies and other bodies, mainly gas and dust. The effects of this explosion are still continuing, causing the universe to expand (right). The galaxies still seem to be rushing away from each other.

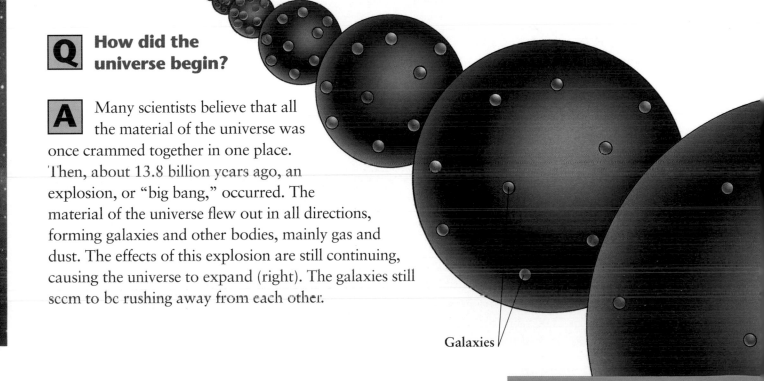

Galaxies

SOLAR SYSTEM

The solar system is made up of the sun, the eight planets—including Earth—that move around it, and millions of smaller objects, such as asteroids.

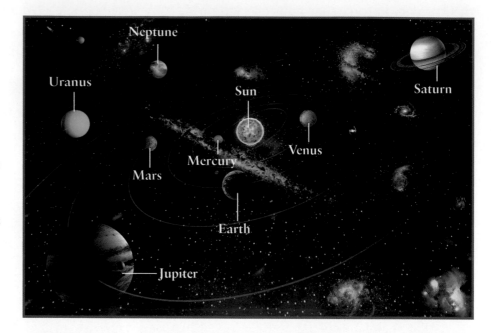

KEY FACTS

Age: The sun probably started to form 4.5 billion years ago

Planets: Eight planets circle the sun

Moons: There are 169 or more moons in the solar system

Rings: The outer planets have rings

Our solar system is just one of many in our galaxy, the Milky Way. The sun is at the center of the solar system. It is a giant ball of gas measuring 865,000 miles (1.39 million km) across.

The Inner Planets

The planets nearest the sun are the terrestrial planets. They are Mercury, Venus, Earth, and Mars. These planets are made mainly of rocks and metals. None of the inner planets have rings, and only Mars and Earth have moons. Earth is the largest of the inner planets, and Mercury is the smallest.

The Outer Planets

The outer planets are the gas giants Jupiter, Saturn, Uranus, and Neptune. They are much bigger

▲ Our solar system includes the sun and the planets that orbit around it. *Solar* means "of the sun."

than the terrestrial planets. Jupiter is large enough to swallow all the other planets, having a diameter of about 88,800 miles (143,000 km). Its mass is more than three hundred times greater than Earth's, though its density is much less.

DISTANCE FROM THE SUN

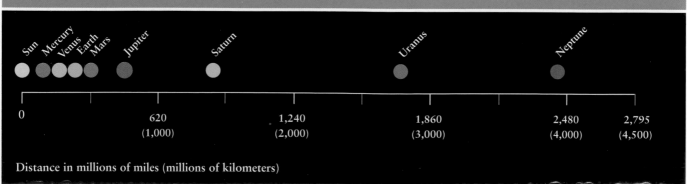

0	620 (1,000)	1,240 (2,000)	1,860 (3,000)	2,480 (4,000)	2,795 (4,500)	

Distance in millions of miles (millions of kilometers)

Ganymede, one of Jupiter's moons, and Titan, one of Saturn's, are both larger than the planet closest to the sun, Mercury.

Comets

Astronomers know of more than four thousand comets, but it is almost certain that there are many, many more in the solar system. Comets are made of ice and dust. As they enter the inner solar system, the ice begins to turn to gas, forming a distinctive tail, or coma.

METEORITES

Meteorites are natural objects from outer space that strike Earth's surface. As they pass through Earth's atmosphere, they become very hot and give off light. In the night sky, they are visible as shooting stars. Depending on what they are made of, meteorites may be stony, iron, or stony-iron.

The orbits of comets are highly variable, but all take a long time to complete. Some may last less than two hundred years, and others may take thousands of years to complete their orbit.

Asteroids

Asteroids are relatively small bodies of rock and ice or metal and rock

▼ When meteorites smash into Earth, they leave holes or craters. Some measure over half a mile (almost a kilometer) across.

that orbit the sun. Most are in the asteroid belt between Mars and Jupiter. Some are very small, but an asteroid called Ceres has a diameter of more than 605 miles (975 km). It is sometimes called a dwarf planet.

◄ A comet blazes across the night sky. The bright head and tail of a comet form when it gets close to the sun.

GENERAL INFORMATION

- The largest planet is Jupiter, and the smallest is Mercury.
- Venus is the hottest planet, and Neptune is the coldest.
- It takes Neptune 165 years to complete an orbit of the sun.
- The sun is composed mostly of hydrogen gas.
- There may be one trillion comets in the solar system.

Altitude
in miles
(km)

60
(95)

- Upper haze

50
(80)

40
(64)

- Upper cloud

- Middle cloud

- Lower cloud

25
(40)

- Lower haze

10
(16)

0

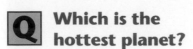

Q Which is the hottest planet?

A Venus. It is the second planet from the sun. Venus is covered in dense clouds (left). These act like a giant greenhouse, raising temperatures to 864° Fahrenheit (462° Celsius). Several probes have landed on Venus, but none have survived.

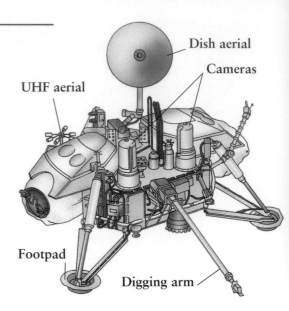

Dish aerial

Cameras

UHF aerial

Footpad

Digging arm

Q Is there life on Mars?

A In 1976, two space probes, *Viking 1* and *Viking 2* (above), landed on Mars and sent pictures of the rocky surface back to Earth. There were no astronauts aboard the *Viking* probes, so automatic soil samplers tested the red, dry soil for any sign of life. None was found.

Q Which planets have rings?

A Jupiter, Saturn, Uranus, and Neptune have rings. The rings are actually tiny pieces of rock covered with ice. Rings may be fragments of moons that were destroyed, or they may have been part of the planets.

Q How large is our sun?

A The sun (below) has a diameter of 865,000 miles (1,392,000 km). Its volume is approximately 1.3 million times larger than Earth's. However, the sun is only a medium-size star; many stars are much bigger. The biggest planet in our solar system is Jupiter (88,846 miles/ 142,984 km diameter), and the smallest is Mercury (3,031 miles/ 4,878 km diameter).

Jupiter

Mercury   Venus   Earth   Mars

Sun

Q How hot is the sun?

A The sun is a vast ball of glowing gas (right). At its heart, temperatures are thought to be 27,000,000°F (15,000,000°C)! The heat is created in the core, or center, by the nuclear fusion of hydrogen atoms. This is similar to the process that occurs in an exploding hydrogen bomb. Marks on the sun, called sunspots, appear dark only because they are 2,192°F (1,200°C) cooler than the surrounding gas. Solar flares are great tongues of gas. All life on Earth is dependent upon the light and heat from the sun.

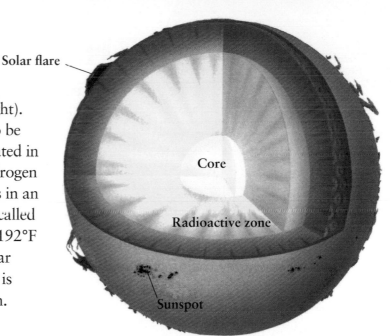

Solar flare

Core

Radioactive zone

Sunspot

Q How do we know so much about the planets?

A Space probes travel through the solar system sending information back to Earth. Space probes carry cameras to take pictures, as well as equipment to detect the presence of radio waves and magnetic fields.

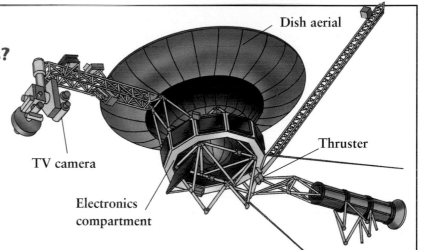

Dish aerial

Thruster

TV camera

Electronics compartment

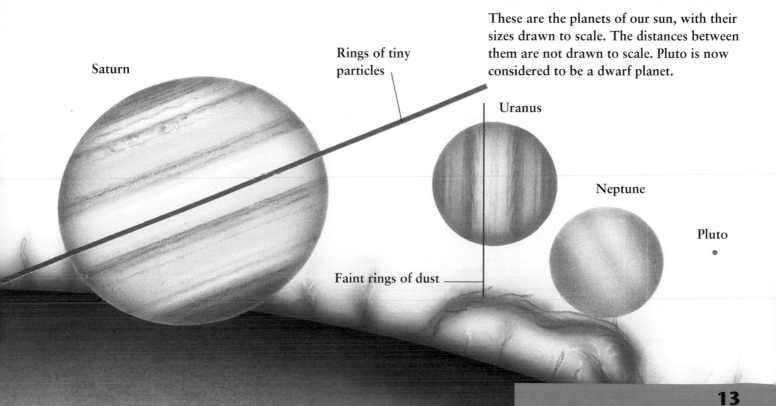

These are the planets of our sun, with their sizes drawn to scale. The distances between them are not drawn to scale. Pluto is now considered to be a dwarf planet.

Saturn

Rings of tiny particles

Uranus

Neptune

Pluto

Faint rings of dust

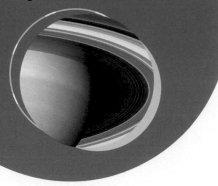

THE PLANETS

There are eight planets in our solar system: the rocky Mercury, Venus, Earth, and Mars, and the gas giants Jupiter, Saturn, Uranus, and Neptune.

KEY FACTS

Smallest: Mercury, diameter 3,032 miles (4,879 km)

Largest: Jupiter, diameter 88,846 miles (142,984 km)

Lightest: Mercury, 5.5 percent of Earth's mass

Heaviest: Jupiter, 318 times Earth's mass

All the planets follow elliptical (oval-shaped) orbits (paths) around the sun. Mercury is the closest planet to the sun. At its nearest, Mercury's orbit brings it to within 28.6 million miles (46 million km) of the sun. Mercury is the smallest of the true planets. Its diameter is only 3,032 miles (4,879 km), half that of Earth's. Mercury has little atmosphere, and its gravity is just one-third that of Earth's. Its ground temperature can rise to a scorching 698°F (370°C).

Venus, the second planet from the sun, is similar in size to Earth and is covered by thick clouds of sulfuric acid. The atmosphere is extremely hot, and there is a lot of volcanic activity.

Earth is the third planet from the sun. Mars is the last of the terrestrial (rocky) planets. Intermediate between Mercury and Earth in size, Mars has only a thin atmosphere

▼ This robotic rover operated on the surface of Mars, the "red planet," between 2004 and 2010.

▲ Jupiter is the biggest planet in the solar system. The Great Red Spot atmospheric storm is visible near the bottom of the image.

and less gravity than Earth. The surface of Mars is a freezing desert with dry and bitterly cold weather.

The Gas Giants

The largest of the planets is the gas giant Jupiter, which has a diameter more than ten times that of Earth—88,846 miles (142,984 km)—and huge gravity. It takes nearly twelve years for Jupiter to orbit the sun. The planet does not have a solid surface. Below an atmospheric mix of hydrogen and other chemicals is a zone of purer hydrogen gas. This merges gradually into an ocean of liquid hydrogen and helium. No one knows for certain what is inside Jupiter's core.

Saturn is huge, though not as enormous as Jupiter, and is the least dense of the planets. Being ten times farther from the sun than Earth, it takes thirty years to complete one orbit. Saturn is best known for its rings. These are bands of millions of lumps of rock and ice. The planet has a small rocky core, surrounded by hydrogen gas and liquid hydrogen and helium.

PLUTO

For many years, Pluto was the ninth planet in the solar system. In 2006, scientists agreed to rename it a "dwarf planet." Pluto is much smaller than the other planets, even smaller than our moon. Its orbit is tilted compared with those of the other planets.

Saturn's surface is racked by constant storms. Although Saturn's surface is much colder than anywhere on Earth, its core may be as hot as the surface of the sun.

The most distant true planets—Uranus and Neptune—are sometimes called ice giants. They are about the same size and mostly made of hydrogen and helium, with some methane. Each one has a solid core; Neptune's is hotter than Uranus's.

▲ An artist's impression of one of Saturn's rings, seen close up.

GENERAL INFORMATION

- Mercury's orbit is the most elliptical, ranging from 29 million miles to 43 million miles (46 million km to 70 million km) from the sun.
- Although it is farther from the sun than Mercury, Venus has the hottest surface temperatures.
- The temperature on the surface of Neptune falls to −328°F (−200°C), making it the coldest planet.

Q What are planets made of?

A The planets that are closest to the sun, from Mercury to Mars, are small, rocky worlds. They have a metal center, or core, surrounded by a thick mantle of rock with a thin, rocky crust on the surface. The outer planets are very different. Jupiter and Saturn are made mostly of hydrogen. Uranus and Neptune have a rock core surrounded by ice, hydrogen, and helium (below).

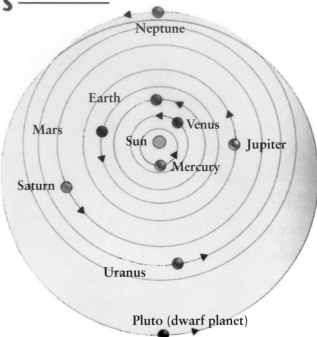

Neptune
Earth
Mars
Venus
Sun
Jupiter
Mercury
Saturn
Uranus
Pluto (dwarf planet)

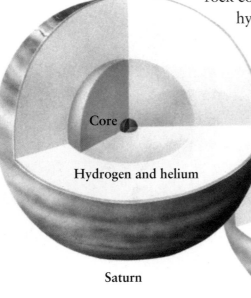

Core
Hydrogen and helium

Saturn

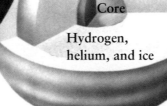

Core
Hydrogen, helium, and ice

Uranus

Q How do the planets orbit the sun?

A All the planets in the solar system travel in the same counterclockwise direction around the sun (above). Their paths are slightly flattened circles called ellipses. Mercury's orbit is the most elliptical.

Q What are planets?

A Planets are worlds that orbit the sun. The word *planet* comes from a Greek word meaning "wanderer," because of the wandering paths they appear to have when seen from Earth. The eight planets (right) are Mercury, Venus, Earth, Mars, Jupiter, Saturn, Uranus, and Neptune. Pluto is now described as a dwarf planet.

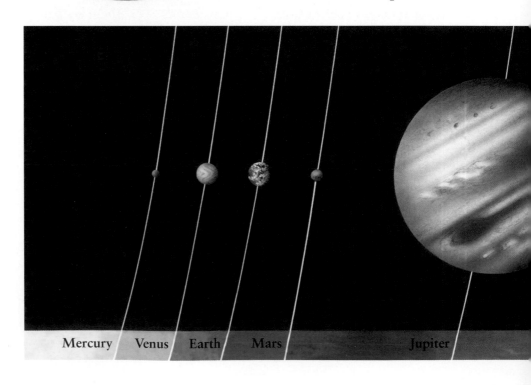

Mercury   Venus   Earth   Mars   Jupiter

Q What is the Great Red Spot?

A Jupiter's Great Red Spot (below) is a swirling storm 18,640 miles (30,000 km) across. It was first seen in 1664. Storms on Earth last a few weeks at most. The Great Red Spot has lasted for centuries because Jupiter has no solid surface to slow the storm down.

Great Red Spot

Q Which planets have moons?

A Only Mercury and Venus do not have moons. Earth has one moon. Mars has two (above). Jupiter has sixty-four moons. One of them, Ganymede, is larger than the planet Mercury. Saturn has sixty-two moons, Uranus twenty-seven, and Neptune thirteen.

Q What are the canals of Mars?

A Over the centuries, astronomers thought that the dark lines and patches on the surface of Mars might be canals, built by an ancient civilization for carrying water. However, none of these so-called canals is visible in photographs taken by probes sent from Earth to Mars. Therefore, scientists now believe that the canals are probably an optical illusion.

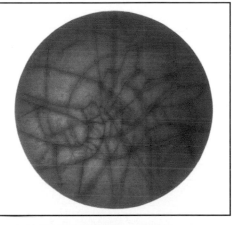

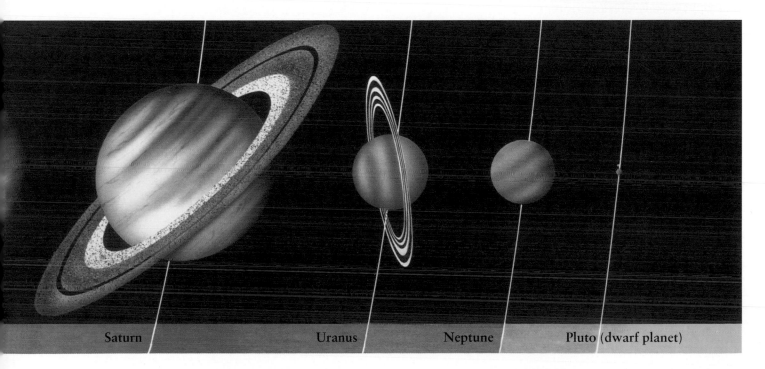

Saturn   Uranus   Neptune   Pluto (dwarf planet)

THE MOON

With a diameter of 2,159 miles (3,475 km), the moon—Earth's only natural satellite—is the fifth biggest moon in the solar system.

▲ This is the far side of the moon, which cannot be seen from Earth. It is sometimes called its "dark side," but it is not always dark.

The moon has hardly any atmosphere, has no weather, and shows no evidence of recent geological activity. Because it has no protective atmosphere, surface temperatures vary greatly, according to whether there is direct sunlight or not. At the moon's equator, temperatures range from –99°F to 243°F (–73°C° to 117°C). It is colder at high latitudes; near the poles, temperatures range from –333°F to –45°F (–203°C to –43°C).

The moon's gravitational force is much weaker than Earth's, though it is still strong enough to exert a pull on Earth's oceans. This causes the tides. Its magnetic field is also much weaker than Earth's.

KEY FACTS

Age: 4.5 billion years
Diameter: 2,159 miles (3,475 km)
Earth orbit: 27.32 days
Solar orbit: 365.26 days

Lunar Orbit

The moon's orbit takes it as close as 221,456 miles (356,400 km) from Earth and as far as 252,712 miles (406,700 km). The moon takes just over twenty-seven days to orbit Earth and always shows the same face to its parent planet.

Because of the changing angle of direct light from the sun, the moon passes through several

ECLIPSES

A lunar eclipse only takes place when the sun, Earth, and the moon are perfectly aligned and Earth is between the other two bodies. Earth's shadow prevents sunlight from reaching the moon, so its luminous disk is extinguished. A solar eclipse is very different. It happens when the moon is perfectly aligned between the sun and Earth, blocking out the sun's light. From Earth, the sun then partially or wholly disappears.

phases during the course of its twenty-seven-day orbit: new moon, waxing crescent, first quarter, waxing gibbous, full moon, waning gibbous, last quarter, and waning crescent. These phases have been known since ancient times, and the first calendars were based on them.

The Moon's Origin

The moon has an inner and outer core, a mantle, and a crust about 30–37 miles (48–60 km) thick.

It is thought that the moon formed from the debris resulting from a collision between two planets about 4.5 billion years ago.

▼ Neil Armstrong was the first person to set foot on the moon, in July 1969.

The Surface

The moon's surface has many craters. With no protective atmosphere, the moon has been hit by lots of meteorites. At least 300,000 large impact craters pepper the surface. There are also lunar plains (maria), formed from pools of solidified lava.

◄ Earth rising over the moon's horizon. The moon is the only body in the solar system that people have visited. There were six manned lunar landings between 1969 and 1972.

GENERAL INFORMATION

● Because of the way it orbits, the same face of the moon always faces Earth. It was only when astronauts were able to orbit the moon in the 1960s that the far side of the moon was seen.

● The center of the moon is made of a solid inner core of iron-rich rock.

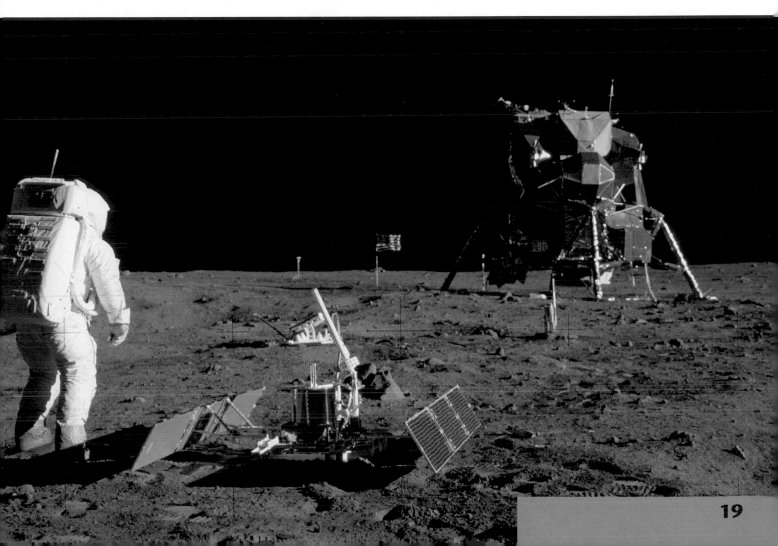

Q Why does the moon seem to change shape?

A The moon shines because it reflects light from the sun. However, as it travels around Earth, we see more or less of its surface, making it appear to change in shape. The different shapes are called phases (below).

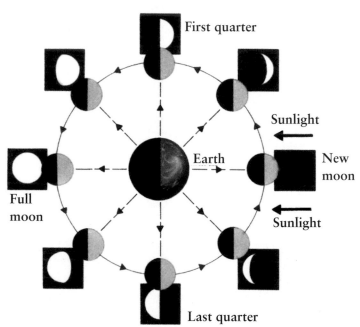

First quarter

Sunlight

Earth

New moon

Full moon

Sunlight

Last quarter

Q What is inside the moon?

A No one has ever examined the inside of the moon (below). Its outside looks very different from Earth's, but inside it is probably similar. Beneath the thin outer crust is a mantle of solid rock. Under this is a thinner layer of molten rock, and at the center is the core, about 876 miles (1,410 km) from the surface.

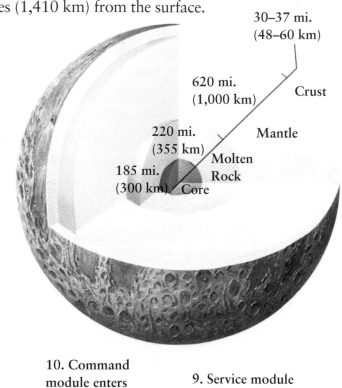

30–37 mi. (48–60 km)

620 mi. (1,000 km)

Crust

Mantle

220 mi. (355 km)

Molten Rock

185 mi. (300 km)

Core

Q When did people first land on the moon?

A The *Apollo 11* spacecraft (right) took off in July 1969. It was carried by a huge Saturn rocket for the first stage of its journey. Shooting out of Earth's orbit, *Apollo 11* traveled to the moon. The lunar module separated and landed on the moon's surface. Two of the crew, Neil Armstrong and Edwin Aldrin, became the first people to walk on the moon.

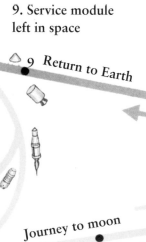

11. Splash down with parachutes

1. *Apollo* takes off

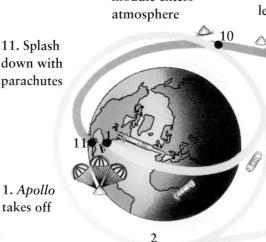

10. Command module enters atmosphere

9. Service module left in space

10

9 Return to Earth

11

2

Journey to moon

3

2. *Apollo* leaves Earth's orbit

3. Prepares for journey to moon

Q What is on the surface of the moon?

A The moon's surface (right) is covered with dust and rocks that have been smashed to pieces by showers of rocklike objects called meteorites. It is pitted with craters, also caused by meteorites. Most are just tiny dents, but some are hundreds of miles wide. Some areas of the moon look dark. People once thought these areas were seas. They were formed when meteorites cracked the moon's surface. Molten rock bubbled up from below and grew hard. There are also many high mountains and deep valleys.

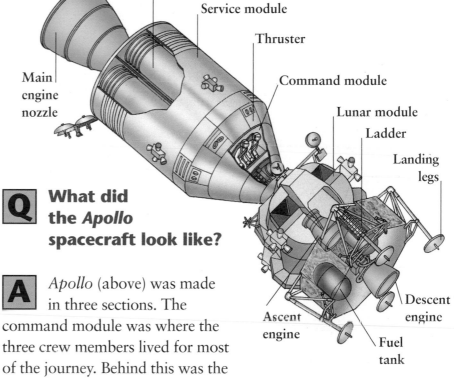

Fuel tank
Service module
Thruster
Command module
Lunar module
Ladder
Landing legs
Main engine nozzle
Descent engine
Ascent engine
Fuel tank

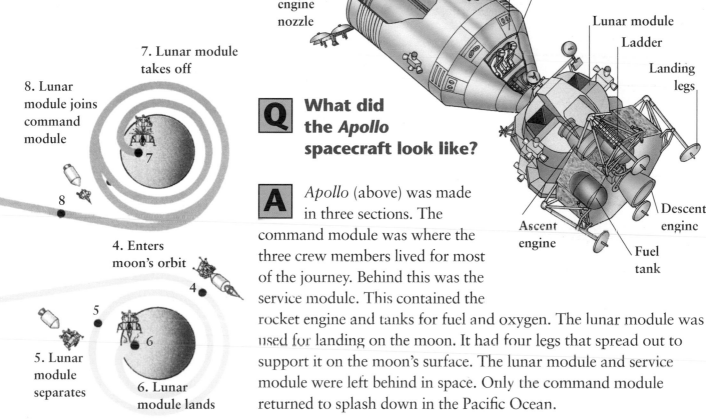

7. Lunar module takes off

8. Lunar module joins command module

8

4. Enters moon's orbit

4

5

6

5. Lunar module separates

6. Lunar module lands

Q What did the *Apollo* spacecraft look like?

A *Apollo* (above) was made in three sections. The command module was where the three crew members lived for most of the journey. Behind this was the service module. This contained the rocket engine and tanks for fuel and oxygen. The lunar module was used for landing on the moon. It had four legs that spread out to support it on the moon's surface. The lunar module and service module were left behind in space. Only the command module returned to splash down in the Pacific Ocean.

EXPLORING THE HEAVENS

For thousands of years, people have been fascinated by the night sky. Until recently, our knowledge depended on observations from Earth.

▲ The seventh-century BCE Venus tablet of Ammisaduqa details Assyrian observations of Venus.

▲ Galileo Galilei demonstrates his telescope in Venice, Italy, in 1609.

The ancient Babylonians, Egyptians, and Greeks made thorough observations. Priests took a particular interest in astronomy, believing that movements of the "celestial bodies" (planets and stars) were signs from the gods. In the third millennium BCE, the Egyptians built pyramids to align with the sun. Astronomy was an important part of their religion. They recorded the phases of the sun, moon, and stars.

The Sumerians (who lived in present-day Iraq) had noted Venus by 1500 BCE, and not long afterward, Babylonian stargazers observed, described, and predicted the movements of Venus, Mercury, Mars, Jupiter, and Saturn. These were the only known planets until the invention of the telescope.

Earth at the Center?

Early people thought that Earth was at the center of the universe, and that the stars and planets moved around it. In the third century BCE, an ancient Greek, Aristarchus of Samos (310–230 BCE), was probably the first to suggest a heliocentric model of the solar system. This meant that the sun, not Earth, was at its center. The heliocentric model was not generally accepted for many centuries. Most people still believed that Earth was at the center of the universe until the idea was challenged in the sixteenth century.

KEPLER SPACE OBSERVATORY

This observatory orbits high above Earth. When it was launched in 2009, its aim was to search for planets outside our own solar system (exoplanets) that could support life. As of late 2014, nearly one thousand of these had been found. Several of them were in "habitable zones" where there was the potential for life. There could be 160 billion exoplanets in the Milky Way galaxy.

Renaissance Discovery

Our understanding of the solar system grew during the Renaissance of the fifteenth to the seventeenth centuries. Copernicus (1473–1543) argued for a heliocentric system for the solar system in 1543. Galileo Galilei (1564–1642) used a telescope to discover the four largest moons orbiting Jupiter.

Expanding Universe

The work of theoretical physicists such as Albert Einstein (1879–1955) helped scientists understand how the universe is changing.

In the late twentieth century, giant telescopes allowed people to see more distant objects. The European Very Large Telescope Array at Cerro Paranal, Chile, has tracked the movement of stars orbiting the huge black hole at the center of the Milky Way galaxy.

▲ An unmanned space probe is launched on a rocket. Space probes now have powerful telescopes to view the universe.

The *Voyager* probes sent to the outer limits of the solar system have added to our knowledge.

GENERAL INFORMATION

- Galileo supported the heliocentric model of the solar system. At the time, this went against the teachings of the Catholic Church, and Galileo spent years under house arrest.

- In 2014, the space probes *Voyager 1* and *Voyager 2* were 12 billion mi. and 9.9 billion mi. (19.4 billion km and 15.9 billion km) from Earth.

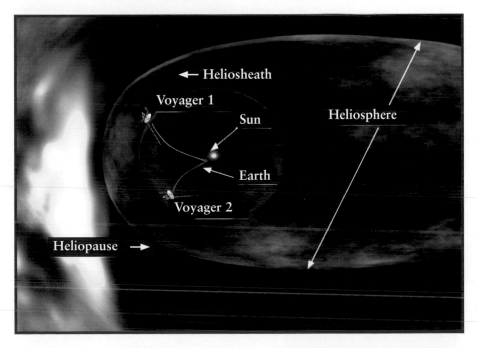

▲ Here, the routes of *Voyager 1* and *Voyager 2* pass through the outer region of our solar system, the heliosheath, and approach its edge, the heliopause.

Q How did early astronomers study the heavens?

A Astronomers studied the sky with the naked eye until the seventeenth century. In 1609, Italian astronomer Galileo Galilei (above) became the first person to study the sky with a telescope.

Q What did *Giotto* tell us about comets?

A In 1986, the *Giotto* space probe (below) studied Halley's Comet. A comet consists of a lump of rock and ice called the nucleus, inside a cloud of gas and dust called the coma (inset). It also has a bright tail. *Giotto*'s photographs show a nucleus measuring 5 miles by 7.5 miles (8 km by 12 km). Its instruments found that the coma and tail are made of dust and water vapor.

Q How does a modern telescope work?

A There are two types of telescope. A refractor uses a lens to form an image. A reflector uses a curved mirror. Most modern telescopes used in astronomy are reflectors. The telescope is finely balanced and turns slowly to keep the image steady as Earth moves. A Schmidt telescope (right) is used to photograph large areas of the sky.

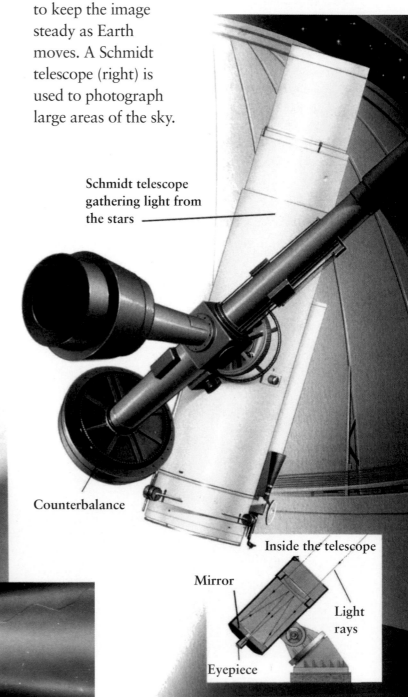

Schmidt telescope gathering light from the stars

Counterbalance

Inside the telescope

Mirror

Light rays

Eyepiece

Q Why is the Hubble Telescope in space?

A Light from distant stars passes through Earth's atmosphere before it reaches a telescope on the ground. The swirling atmosphere makes the stars twinkle. Modern telescopes are usually built on top of mountains, where the atmosphere is thinner, to reduce this effect. The Hubble Space Telescope (below) can see more clearly than any telescope on Earth because it is above the atmosphere.

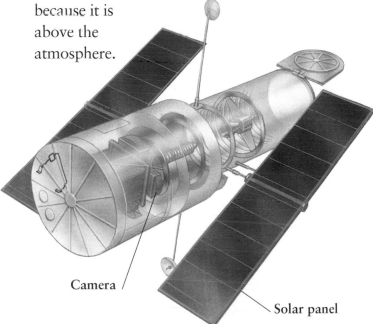

Camera

Solar panel

Q Where did the *Voyager* space probes go?

A *Voyager 1* and *Voyager 2* were launched in 1977. The pull of gravity from the outer planets guided the spacecraft from one planet to the next. *Voyager 1* flew past Jupiter in 1979 (below) and Saturn in 1980. *Voyager 2* flew past Jupiter (1979), Saturn (1981), Uranus (1986), and Neptune (1989). Their cameras and instruments studied each planet. All the information was sent back to Earth by radio.

Q How did the *Pioneer* space probes work?

A *Pioneer 10* and *11* (right), launched in 1972 and 1973, were the first spacecraft to visit the outer solar system. They were designed to find out if a spacecraft could travel through the asteroid belt, a swarm of rocks orbiting the sun between Mars and Jupiter. Most spacecraft use solar cells to make electricity from sunlight. *Pioneer 10* and *11* traveled so far from the sun that solar cells would not work. Instead, they carried nuclear power generators to make electricity.

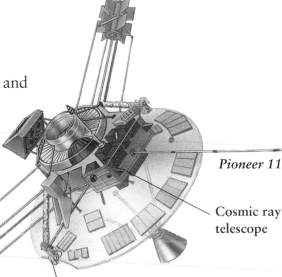

Pioneer 11

Cosmic ray telescope

Thruster

Nuclear power generator

SPACE TRAVEL

Space travel was the dream of science fiction writers before the rocket technology developed in World War II began to make it a reality.

American scientists used German V2 rocket designs to launch rockets into the upper levels of Earth's atmosphere. One rocket reached the height of 250 miles (400 km) in 1950.

The Space Race

The 1950s and 1960s were dominated by the "space race"—furious competition between the former Soviet Union and the United States. The Soviet Union scored the first successes. *Sputnik 1*, launched in 1957, was the first human-made object to orbit Earth. Soon after, the Soviets put the first animal—Laika the dog—into orbit. In 1961, Russian cosmonaut Yuri Gagarin (1934–1968) became the first person to go into space, completing a full orbit around Earth. Four years later, Alexey Leonov (b. 1934) performed the first walk in space.

The Apollo Missions

From the mid-1960s, the United States' Apollo program was very successful. The *Apollo 8* mission was the first to orbit the moon, then on July 20, 1969, *Apollo 11* landed astronauts Neil Armstrong (1930–2012) and Edwin "Buzz" Aldrin (b. 1930) on its surface. But after six missions to take people to the moon, the program ended.

Going Farther Afield

The emphasis switched to unmanned probes and space stations. US space agency NASA's

▲ In 1961, Russian astronaut Yuri Gagarin was the first person to complete a full orbit of Earth.

▼ One of the American space shuttles lands after a mission to the International Space Station.

KEY FACTS

First manned space flight:
April 12, 1961, Yuri Gagarin

First space walk:
March 18, 1965, Alexey Leonov

First manned orbit of the moon: December 14, 1968, Frank Borman, James Lovell, and William Anders

First people on the moon:
July 21, 1969, Neil Armstrong and Edwin "Buzz" Aldrin

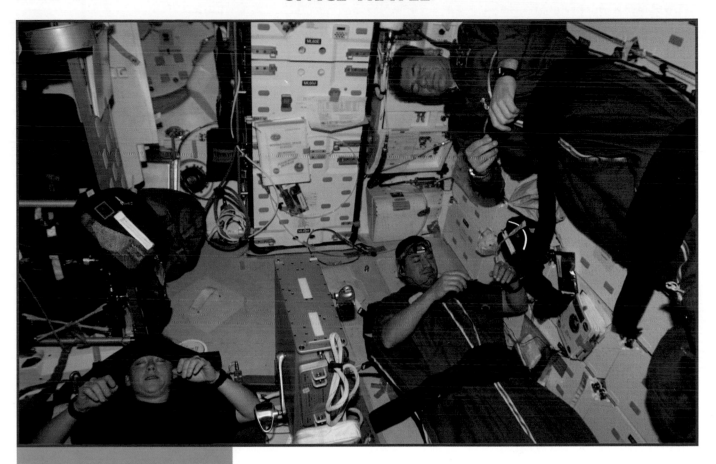

THE SPACE STATION

The International Space Station (ISS) is a collaboration between the United States, Russia, Europe, Japan, and Canada. The US space agency NASA used five space shuttles—the first reusable spacecraft—to get astronauts there and back from 1981 to 2011. The ISS will operate until 2020 at least. In its first ten years, the ISS traveled 1.5 billion miles (2.4 billion km)—57,361 orbits around Earth.

Mariner, Pioneer, and Voyager probes made many discoveries. Flybys of the planets began in 1962 when *Mariner 2* passed Venus, and *Mariner 4* approached Mars in 1965. The pace then picked up: *Pioneer 10* passed close to Jupiter in 1973,

Mariner 10 did a flyby of Mercury in 1974, and *Pioneer 11* approached Saturn in 1979.

More Distant Planets

Much more recently, the *Cassini* spacecraft went into orbit around Saturn in 2004, and a lander craft has sent back information from the surface of Titan, one of its moons.

The *Voyager 1* and *Voyager 2* unmanned probes have now gone far beyond Pluto. In 2014, the probes were traveling at great speed and *Voyager 1* had reached interstellar space—the region between stars.

Commercial space travel began in 2001. Since then, small numbers of space tourists have been able to visit the International Space Station, but the flights are very expensive.

▲ Scientists in the International Space Station, which orbits Earth at a height of 205–255 miles (330–410 km). The crew comes from different countries.

GENERAL INFORMATION

- The US Apollo program ran from 1961 to 1972. Its goal was "landing a man on the moon and returning him safely to Earth." This happened in 1969. The program cost $24 billion.

- Teams of astronauts have occupied the International Space Station (ISS) continuously since November 2000. During that time, more than two hundred individuals of fifteen different nationalities have visited.

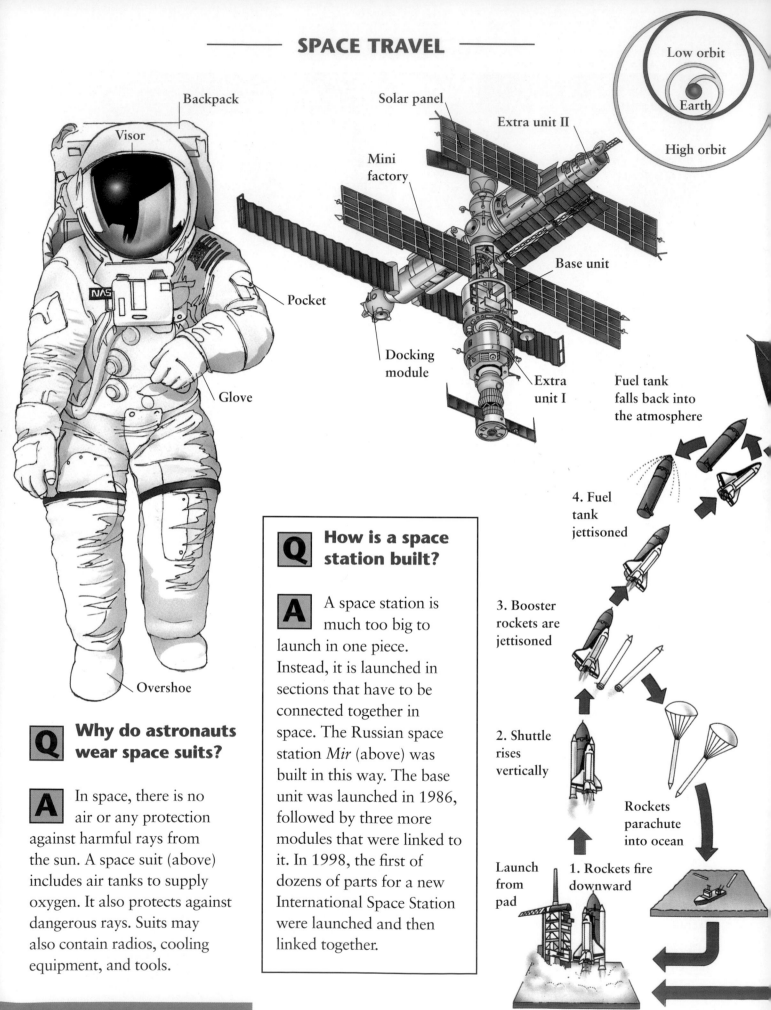

Backpack

Visor

Solar panel

Extra unit II

Low orbit

Earth

High orbit

Mini factory

Pocket

Base unit

Docking module

Glove

Extra unit I

Fuel tank falls back into the atmosphere

4. Fuel tank jettisoned

3. Booster rockets are jettisoned

Overshoe

Q Why do astronauts wear space suits?

A In space, there is no air or any protection against harmful rays from the sun. A space suit (above) includes air tanks to supply oxygen. It also protects against dangerous rays. Suits may also contain radios, cooling equipment, and tools.

Q How is a space station built?

A A space station is much too big to launch in one piece. Instead, it is launched in sections that have to be connected together in space. The Russian space station *Mir* (above) was built in this way. The base unit was launched in 1986, followed by three more modules that were linked to it. In 1998, the first of dozens of parts for a new International Space Station were launched and then linked together.

2. Shuttle rises vertically

Rockets parachute into ocean

Launch from pad

1. Rockets fire downward

Q What is an orbit?

A An orbit is the path an object takes around a star, planet, or moon. Satellites circle Earth in several different orbits (left). Those that take photographs use low orbits. High orbits are used by satellites that transmit signals such as television broadcasts.

Q How was the shuttle different from most spacecraft?

A Most spacecraft fly only once, and their rockets burn up in flight. The space shuttle (below) was unusual because the craft and booster rockets could be used again. This meant scientists could spend money on equipment that would have been too expensive to use only once. Satellites were stored in the payload bay for use in orbit. Orbiting satellites could be put into the bay and brought back to Earth for repair.

Q How do spacecraft get into space?

A To enter space, rockets must escape Earth's gravity. This requires a speed of 17,400 miles an hour (28,000 kmh). Such speeds are easiest to reach by vertical takeoff. But it takes huge amounts of power to lift a spacecraft. The space shuttle has a big fuel tank and two booster rockets to supply this power.

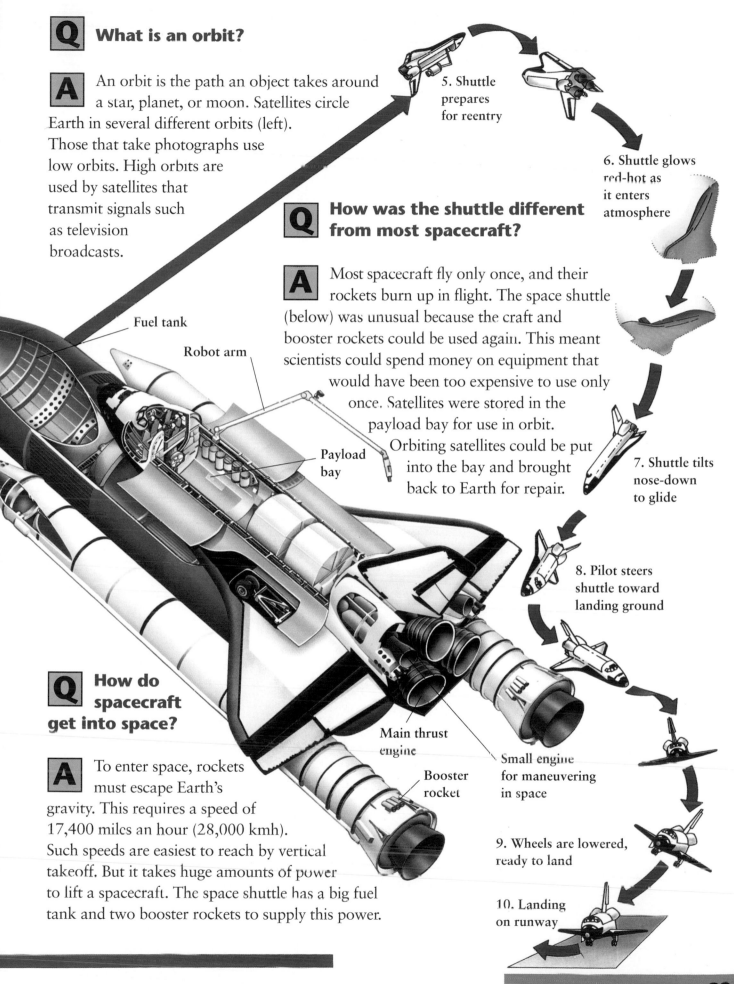

Fuel tank

Robot arm

Payload bay

Main thrust engine

Booster rocket

Small engine for maneuvering in space

5. Shuttle prepares for reentry

6. Shuttle glows red-hot as it enters atmosphere

7. Shuttle tilts nose-down to glide

8. Pilot steers shuttle toward landing ground

9. Wheels are lowered, ready to land

10. Landing on runway

GLOSSARY

big bang theory A theory that says a cosmic explosion called the "big bang" gave birth to the universe.

black hole An area of space with so much gravity that light cannot escape it.

comet A celestial object that has a core of ice and dust. When it is near the sun, a tail of gas and dust trails behind it.

diameter A straight line passing from one side to the other across the middle of a circle or sphere, such as a planet.

heliocentric Something that has the sun at its center, such as the solar system.

galaxy A collection of millions of stars held together by gravity.

gas giant A large planet made up mainly of the gases hydrogen and helium. Jupiter, Saturn, Uranus, and Neptune are gas giants.

light year The distance light travels in a year, about 6,000,000,000,000 (6 trillion) miles (9.6 trillion km).

meteor A particle of dust that enters Earth's atmosphere and is visible as a streak of light or "shooting star."

Milky Way The galaxy to which Earth belongs. It is made up of vast numbers of stars and appears as a faint band of light across the sky.

moon A natural body that orbits a planet, such as Earth's moon.

nebula A cloud made up of gas and dust in outer space, visible from Earth as a patch of bright light.

orbit The curved path of something around a planet, moon, or star.

dwarf planet A celestial body too small to be called a planet. In our solar system, Pluto is a dwarf planet.

solar system A group of planets and their moons, plus asteroids and comets, that orbit around a sun. Our solar system has eight planets.

spacecraft A vehicle that is used for traveling in space, such as the Apollo rockets or the Voyager space probes.

space probe An unmanned spacecraft used to collect information about its environment and send it back to Earth.

space station An orbiting spacecraft that is manned and designed to stay in space.

reflector A telescope that uses a curved mirror to make distant objects look nearer.

refractor A telescope that uses a lens to make stars and planets look nearer.

universe All space and matter; all the galaxies and everything in them.

FURTHER READING

Books

Aguilar, David A. *Space Encyclopedia: A Tour of Our Solar System and Beyond.* Washington, DC: National Geographic Children's Books, 2013.

Chaikin, Andrew. *Mission Control, This is Apollo: The Story of the First Voyages to the Moon.* New York: Viking Juvenile, 2009.

DK Publishing. *Space: A Visual Encyclopedia.* New York: DK Publishing, 2010.

Racine, Shirley, and Kathi Wagner. *The Everything Kids' Astronomy Book.* Avon, MA: Adams Media, 2008.

Stott, Carole. *Space Exploration.* New York: DK Publishing, 2009.

Websites

NASA's Space Place
spaceplace.nasa.gov
This fantastic site helps you explore the sun, moon, Earth, and other planets in our solar system. With games, activities, and science projects that make learning about space fun and exciting!

National Geographics Space Portal
news.nationalgeographic.com/space
Check out the latest news from outer space on this amazing site, with information on space missions, galaxies, meteor showers, and other sky events. Full of awesome photos and videos of galaxies, stars, spacecraft, solar storms, and more!

Smithsonian National Air and Space Museum
airandspace.si.edu/explore-and-learn/topics
Catch live views of the sky from Smithsonian's telescopes, and learn all about the history of astronomy, the space shuttle, Mars, and the Apollo program.

INDEX